ZEN ROHATSU

ZEN ROHATSU

BY NORA D'ECCLESIS

Published by Renaissance Presentations, LLC
King of Prussia, PA

ISBN: 978-1-7330201-3-8

Library of Congress Control Number: 2022911744

1st Edition: July, 2022

Dedication

To Janice L. Prodell, with gratitude for your grace, compassion and friendship. Thank you for sitting zazen meditation with me over the years since our first meeting sitting upright on zafus.

Table of Contents

Spiritual Path to Enlightenment
A Guided Visualization...

Rohatsu begins with the sound of an ancient gong, and the scent of incense permeating the zendo as we enter the spiritual practice. Mindfully walking, one hand closed, the other covering it in shashu, feeling each step and the precision of our movement. Circumambulating as the Buddha did thousands of years ago. From the first step when the ball of the big toe hits the ground, we unite the walking meditation with zazen bringing the stillness of sitting in meditation into action.

We stay in the present. We are not thinking of anything. We are mindful. Each step is breathing in and breathing out in synergy with our kinhin.

We rise from zazen seated meditation by tilting the torso forward upright about ninety degrees, then extending the hips and knees. We stand on a mid-foot landing, letting go of everything and controlling the breath as we move forward in peace and equanimity. Kinhin as our walking meditation is practiced with our eyes at half-mast looking not at the walls of the zendo or the birds in the trees through the window.

When we hear a sound, we simply hear it, so the chirping bird does not excite us and break the walking meditation, nor does the fire truck racing down the street with sirens blaring. We do not look up or take note to tell the other meditators how lovely the sound of the bird. We allow the concept of bird chirping then proceed in kinhin. While walking indoors we might be tempted to cut corners, but this is not best, as Zens do not cut corners in the walking meditation or in life.

Walking now, one foot extending in front of the other, mindfully walking as we meditate with others in a community of spirituality. Today is the day we will exit the solitude of the meditation hall as we walk single file out the door and move toward an outdoor walking meditation.

Visualize a huge labyrinth similar to the one in Notre Dame de Chartres in Paris. Our labyrinth sits at the foot of a snow-capped mountain in an area of lush trees and gardens. It might be said that walking into a labyrinth is a metaphor for walking toward your core. It is a spiritual experience.

Our labyrinth is unicursal; when you walk in and around, the way out is exactly the same as the way in. It is not a maze or puzzle to be solved; a labyrinth is a path in and out. As we walk in silent meditation into the labyrinth, we pause at the entrance to center ourselves. We encounter other people on the parallel paths. The journey might seem long one time and very short the next. We might be so intent on getting to the end that we miss the subtle sounds, sights, smells of nature. If we are mindful, we notice the small signs that others have passed this way before us as a footprint, a memento left lovingly behind, a stone dislodged by a wayward boot. We notice our inclination to make everything perfect again, pick up the stone, erase the footprint.

We acknowledge the sacredness of the space, cleansed by many feet silently stepping, spiraling through the small path. We feel the connection to all who have traveled this path, and especially to those on it together in community meditation, our sangha. We then return to the meditation center with intention set toward our more spiritual core and the silence of seated meditation. Satori, or the experience of awakening, is a little closer.

Zen Rohatsu
The Backstory Of Why We Meditate

Rohatsu is a spiritual practice of meditative zazen that occurs on the eighth day of the twelfth month on the Gregorian calendar. The meditation sessions, which focus on zazen rather than scriptures or rituals, are celebrated for seven days in advance of December 8th by Zen practitioners all over the world. The Rohatsu days and nights are replicated enactments of how we think historical Buddha from the Shakyamuni tribe achieved enlightenment. As we enter the zendo, monks explain the logistics of the week and silent meditation. It includes a look at why Buddha sat in front of that banyan fig tree known as a peepul tree in Bodh Gaya in India.

Zen is but one branch of the Buddhist tree that emerged as a result of those eight days, many years ago before written word. We will sit on zafus (small pillows) and zabutons (larger pillows) during the days and evenings of meditation. Bells will inform us when to rise into walking meditations called kinhin. Bells will also inform us of dharma classes and sangha eating times. A Roshi or leader wearing a rokusu will lead us in chanting and dokusan, or personal chats with a monk.

The rokusu worn by Zen monk and master is a replica of a garment worn by the Buddha as he sat to achieve enlightenment. Its purpose then was to keep the Buddha warm as he looked out over a rice field with its rectangular patchwork. It is a patchwork sewn together, traditionally black with a white back and sewn by those preparing to take the Zen precepts or be ordained. The Bodhi Tree or tree of awakening is the sacred fig tree believed to be where the Buddha attained enlightenment. The ficus religiosa banyan fig tree was located in Bodh Gaya.

The meditators will probably sit and eat and sleep on tatami mats for the duration of the session. The food bowls will include a spoon and fork which will be traditionally wrapped in a cloth about 40 centimeters. There will also be a twenty centimeter cloth for cleaning the bowls of food tea after each use. There is an evening prayer before meals and chanting which moves quickly and is dominated by the strong voices of the monks in leadership and training. The eight days will also include Dokusan, which is time alone with the Roshi Zen Master or senior monks to discuss

Zen concepts as they apply to individuals. Work practice is time to clean the zendo each day and is done, like everything else, in silence.

The monks might assign a koan to participants, or time for writing of haiku and calligraphy. The koan is a question usually asked in Zen practice to act as a catalyst to promote doubt. It can be seen as not answerable and always explores non-duality. For example, Hakuin asks in one very famous koan: "*Two hands clap and there is a sound, what is the sound of one hand?*" The goal is for the student of Zen to see themselves apart of the activity, looking for answers to koans resulting in distinct and separate are basically false. That is the insight. Enlightenment and escape from suffering totally is in the hands of the person, who holds the ultimate responsibility.

Dharma classes will teach the Zen masters and their wisdom. Zen Master Dogen Zenji (1200-1253), who founded the *Soto School of Zen* in Moon in the Dewdrop, teachings the important concepts of *beginners mind* in Zen. On the teachings of Zen Master Dogen, he taught of Shikantaza: *"nothing but sitting."* We will learn of translations that taught his concept of Shikantaza including *"It is a state of brightly alert attention that is free of thoughts, directed to no object, and attached to no particular contents,"* and *"Commitment to Zen is casting off body and mind."* Dogen said: *"You have no need for incense, offerings, homage, penance of disciples of silent sutra reading... just sit single-mindedly"* (Collcutt, 49-50).

Another amazing Dharma class might include: *Rohatsu Exhortations* by Zen Master Hakuin Ekaku Zenji (1685-1768), which is read for all to learn more of the world famous Koan author of *"What is the sound of one hand clapping?"* Zen Master Zenji also used calligraphy and painting as visual dharma.

The concept of Karma is sometimes taught in a Dharma class and one of the best definitions comes from a Tibetan named Michael Roach in his book, *The Diamond Cutter* (named for a Sutra of Buddha's teachings): *"When you see yourself helping out an employee who's having a hard time, a good imprint is made in your mind. When you see yourself telling a lie to a customer, a bad imprint is made in your mind."*

Karma is neither inherited nor passed down in any way. Karma is to set intention and the way in which that intention manifests from thought, verbal or physical determines the karma down the road; perhaps many years down the road.

This is the story of how the concept of Buddhist enlightenment emerged from the Buddha's days on earth. Rohatsu is unique to Mahayana Zen — Japanese Zen which celebrates the Rohatsu experience. It is an introduction to the practice. We learn from this historical perspective of what motivated Siddhartha's experience and the men and women who ultimately expanded it globally to share the experience. Buddha was a man who found his enlightenment and set his path, avoiding suffering by controlling his thoughts and desires. He was not and is not considered a deity. The concept of nirvana is an end to suffering, or as he called it, Dukkha. Buddha always replied, according to ancient verbal communications, *"I am awake."* The Buddha was driven by the concept that actions determined merit rather than being born into the higher caste system. It was later recorded in the Vasettha Sutta.

From *The Middle Length Discourses of the Buddha:*

One is not a brahmin by birth,
Nor by birth a non-brahmin.
By action is one a brahmin,
By action is one a non-brahmin

The Life Of Buddha
Sage of the Shaka Clan

Zen is a spiritual path that allows us to experience our essence, opening a portal to view life spontaneously. The meditative path is a journey toward the sacredness of existence. It is said we can all be serenely zen on a mountain during idyllic vacation, but true enlightenment is replicating that during the stress of our daily lives in the workplace, in family relationships and our internal anxiety with daily life. Zen is a Japanese division of Buddhist practice, originating approximately 2,700 years ago.

Who was this man we call Buddha and how did he formulate his ideas and philosophy known as the *Middle Path*? Buddha was the son of Queen Maha Maya and King Suddhodana, who owned the municipality of Kapilavastu in an area that is now known as Nepal. Late in life, the queen realized she was with child and with great joy informed her husband. Maya wanted to return to her parents home to give birth, as it was the custom. The king agreed and made the arrangements for his queen to travel in royal style. On the way to the Koliya country, the great procession passed a garden called Lumbini Park. This garden was near the kingdom of Lumbini Park, at the foot of the Nepal Himalayan Mountains. It was very warm and Queen Maya decided to go wading into a lake. Shortly after that, she went into labor and while holding the branches of a tree, she gave birth to son who would be named Siddhartha Gautama.

The birth took place on a full moon in late May, which is now celebrated as Vesak, the festival of the triple event of Buddha's birth, enlightenment and death in approximately the year 623 BCE. This date is still in question and subject to much debate. The times of Gautama's birth and death are uncertain: most historians in the early twentieth century dated his lifetime as circa 563 BCE to 483 BCE, but more recent opinion dates his death to between 486 and 483 BCE or, according to some, between 411 and 400 BCE. However, at a symposium on this question held in 1988, the majority of those who presented definite opinions gave dates within twenty years either side of 400 BCE for the Buddha's death. These alternative chronologies, however, have not yet been accepted by all other historians (Schumann, 15).

After the birth of her baby son, Queen Maha Maya immediately returned to Kapilavastu to present the king his son. The infant was given the name Siddhartha Gautama in Pāli: Siddhartha, meaning "he who achieves his aim." Seven days after her return home Queen Maya died.

Siddhartha was born into a royal Hindu family and many helped care for him. He was brought up by his mother's younger sister, Maha Pajapati. The king was devastated and called for advice from his advisors to help him understand why the joyful birth of his son caused the death of his wife. The king also wanted to know what type of life his new child would have and how he should raise him, so he called for Asita, a hermit who was ascetic and had great psychic powers. Asita predicted that the Prince Siddhartha of Kapilavastu would either become a great king — called a chakravartin — or become a spiritual leader and Buddha. The king did everything he could think of to be certain his son Prince Siddhartha would grow up prepared for a life following in his own footsteps and become a king of the municipality. The prince was taught math, archery and fighting skills as a young child, but always showed signs of compassion and refused to hunt.

When he reached the age of 16, the king arranged the prince's marriage to a cousin of the same age named Yasodhara. It is said he did so because the future Buddha was so kind and gentle and his uncles suggested he needed a wife. The young prince and princess enjoyed a charmed life so important to the future Buddha's story. He lived in total luxury. It is during this time that Siddhartha's philosophy of life was formed.

Of his luxurious life as a prince he states: *"I was delicate, excessively delicate. In my father's dwelling, three lotus ponds were made purposely for me. Blue lotuses bloomed in one, red in another, and white in the third. I used no sandwood that was not of Kasi. My turban, tunic, dress and cloak were all from Kasi. Night and day a white parasol was held over me so that I might not be touched by heat or cold, dust leaves or dew. There were three palaces built for me- one for the cold season, one for the hot season, one for the rainy season. During the four rainy months, I lived in the palace for the rainy season, entertained by female musicians, without coming down from the palace. Just as in the houses of others, food from the husks of rice together with sour gruel is given to the slaves and workmen, even so, in my father's dwelling, food with rice and meat was given to the slaves and workmen."* —From *A Manual of Buddhism* (Narada).

Siddhartha's life from childhood was spent with a highly competitive cousin named Devadatta. This cousin was divisive and jealous of everything from archery competitions to his wife's hand in marriage. The compassionate way in which Buddha interacted with Devadatta is a testimonial to his character.

We begin to see a pattern of the future Buddha growing bored with the ostentatious lifestyle of his father. However, his father was a great king who treated all humans well in a time when that was not the norm. Prince Siddhartha starts to question the meaning of life and what lies beyond the walls of Kapilavastu at about the same time Yasodhara got pregnant after all those years. According to the history, she gave birth to a son named Rahula who was named by his father, the future historical Buddha. It is interesting to note the meaning of the name Rahula is a soft fetter or chain. Siddhartha is said to have spent twenty-nine years as a prince in Kapilavastu.

Although his father ensured that Siddhartha was provided with everything he could want or need, Buddhist scriptures say that the future Buddha felt that materialism was not what gave his life meaning. The prince requested that his father permit him to enter the city on the other side of the wall. The prince went on a journey and saw old age for the first time. When the prince saw the old man, he didn't know what was wrong with this man. It was the first time in his life that he had been permitted to see an old person. The next sighting was of a man crying out in pain in a scream. This made the prince very sad.

Channa, who was Siddhartha's friend, tried to explain that everyone in this world will eventually get sick, old and die. Buddha asks, *"Why does a man lie there so still, allowing people to burn him? It's as if he does not know anything."* Channa explained the man was dead. Channa explained that the happy men walking around smiling were monks seeking spiritual truths. The Buddha thought that perhaps he would like being a monk. The prince felt very happy now and decided to become a monk. He walked until he was tired, then sat under a tree to think some more. As he was sitting under the cool shady tree, news came that his wife had given birth to a fine baby boy. Siddhartha felt the baby to be an impediment, Rahula had been born and he felt him to be an obstacle to leaving the palace for his spiritual quest.

Siddhartha was determined to leave anyway, so Channa prepared his horse and Siddhartha went to see his newborn son for the first time. His wife was sleeping with the baby beside her. The prince decided to go without waking them to finish what he was looking for and he felt that at some point he would return. Prince Siddhartha left his father's estate, took off his robes and cut his hair to two fingers breath because any shorter and the sun would have burned his head during his walking travels. He became known as ascetic Gautama. He walked all over Northern India for almost six years, fasting and seeking enlightenment, living mostly alone as the ascetics did.

Siddhartha decided to sit under a banyan tree to meditate. He was very weak and he remembered sitting under a tree as a child and feeling very spiritual. It is said that a young woman named Sujata saw him and offered sweet thick milk rice in a golden bowl. When he finished, he took the golden bowl and threw it in the river. He felt if this bowl floated upstream he would give up the path of asceticism. The golden bowl went upstream keeping in the middle of the river. He decided at that moment to sit and meditate until he was enlightened. After he sat for days and faced his demons including a devil-like creature called Mara, Buddha grabbed some earth and proclaimed he achieved enlightenment.

The first teaching ever given by Shakyamuni Buddha was to his first five student monks in Deer Park. The Buddha spoke of the *Four Noble Truths* he had discovered while struggling for enlightenment: these are the central teachings of Buddhism. They provide an ethical and meditative way of life to avoid suffering. The path is called the *Eightfold Path* and is presented here in its entirety.

THE FOUR NOBLE TRUTHS

1. Life means suffering.

During our lifetime we experience illness, injuries, failures, the aging process and finally death. There is suffering along the way as well as joy. Accepting the inevitable loss of our expectations that things will go smoothly almost perfect we realize that life has many degrees of suffering. The suffering is called Dukkha: a nagging dissatisfaction.

2. The origin of suffering is attachment and desire.

We all crave and cling to the materialistic things we desire such as wealth as a goal in and of a goal as itself, as well as attaching to transient imperfect pursuits of fame and popularity. The attachment is to impermanent things and living exists in an impermanent nature.

3. The cessation of suffering is attainable.

The suffering to which we submit ourselves can cease to exist by becoming dispassionate. Equanimity removes the suffering and allows us to maintain a dispassionate life devoid of the ups and downs. We become observers of life without the manic or depressed responses.

4. There is a path to cessation of suffering.

As described by the Buddha it is called The Eight-fold Path to a middle place. It is living our lives without excessive self-indulgence or asceticism. The Noble Eightfold Path as described by Siddhartha Gautama or historical Buddha helps us to understand a moral, ethical and meditative journey to live our lives learning to be content in the chaos. The entire middle path principles are inter-dependent in symbiotic relationship with each other.

THE STEPS OF THE EIGHTFOLD PATH

WISDOM PATH

1. Right View

Or **Understanding** is to see things as they really are. We should stay in the present, being in the moment at all times.

2. Right Intention

To set intention to avoid anger, violence and desires. Not having thoughts of greed and anger.

MORALITY AND ETHICS

3. Right Speech

Avoid lying, gossip, harsh speech, slander and saying hurtful things.

4. Right Action

Similar to the golden rule. Do no harm to others, no killing, no stealing, no over indulging, no excessive drugs or alcoholism, no intoxicating substances, no attention seeking. Not to destroy any life, not to steal or commit adultery. Jukai or "Taking the Precepts" in Buddhism structures right action (this is frequently taken at the end of Rohatsu).

5. **Right Livelihood**

Avoiding occupations that bring harm to oneself and others. Earn wealth legally and peacefully, no arms dealing, no prostitution, no raising animals for slaughter, no slave trade, no drug dealing, no just war, no abattoir, no executioner. However, Buddha was very clear it is not proper to tell anyone what they do is wrong.

MENTAL DISCIPLINE

6. **Right Effort**

Earnestly doing one's best in the right direction. Work on yourself to get rid of improper attitudes. This requires self-discipline.

7. **Right Mindfulness**

Always being aware and attentive, living our lives in the moment and being mindful. For example, when we are eating, just eat.

8. **Right Concentration**

Making the mind steady and calm in order to realize the true nature of things by meditating. All of the Buddhist meditations have value and should be practiced. Kinhin, a walking meditation, and zazen or shikantaza seated meditation mostly on zafu and zabuton pillows.

They sit to achieve *SATORI OR ENLIGHTENMENT.* Buddhists believe that following the Eightfold Path leads, ultimately, to a life free of suffering. Taking the Precepts is a ceremony in Buddhism where people commit to the principles of the Noble Path and the three pure precepts and the ten grave precepts.

THE THREE PURE PRECEPTS

1. Not Creating Evil

2. Practicing Good

3. Actualizing Good For Others

THE TEN GRAVE PRECEPTS

1. Affirm life; Do not kill

2. Be giving; Do not steal

3. Honor the body; Do not misuse sexuality

4. Manifest truth; Do not lie

5. Proceed clearly; Do not cloud the mind

6. See the perfection; Do not speak of others errors and faults

7. Realize self and other as one; Do not elevate the self and blame others

8. Give generously; Do not be withholding

9. Actualize harmony; Do not be angry

10. Experience the intimacy of things; Do not defile the Three Treasures

Soon after the Buddha achieved enlightenment, the first sangha was organized.

Ananda requested that Buddha's former wife and mother of his son be permitted to achieve enlightenment. Buddha's mother who raised him also asked to enter the sangha. After much discussion and three negative responses due to the Buddha's trepidation regarding women walking the paths in the forest alone, he agreed, though with some restrictions. Thus, his mother and wife entered the sangha. They became nuns with many of the rights and privileges of the monks. There was also a short encounter with his father the king who had sent his grandson down to where Buddha was camping to ask for his inheritance. The child did that and within minutes of meeting his father, asked to enter the sangha to achieve enlightenment. Near death, Buddha's father finally understood and achieved enlightenment.

Two of the most famous Dharma teachings include: *The Mustard Seed* and *The Parable of the Poison Arrow*.

The Mustard Seed teaches us how of a young woman, a mother, carried a lifeless child to the Buddha and requested that Buddha bring the child back to life. The Buddha, showing compassion, told the woman to go to the village and bring back some mustard seed from a home that had not seen death. She did that, soon realized the teaching, and even in grief she joined the Sangha.

The Parable of the Poison Arrow teaches the lesson of the futility of asking questions and more questions. A person is shot by a poison arrow but before he or she allows friends to remove the arrow, the person shot asks questions: *Who shot the arrow? Why did they shoot me with an arrow? Which direction did it come from?* It is highly probable the person shot would die before his questions were ever answered.

Buddha walked the earth for almost eighty years and much has been written recently which can be studied in Zen monasteries around the world. Devadatta also followed his cousin into the sangha in an attempt to either control the Buddha's world or end the Buddha's life. Devadatta died trying.

In the Buddha's eighth decade at around age 83, he went north to the Ganges basin with his sangha to avoid the internal wars in India. Many believe the Buddha's health was deteriorating, making it difficult to walk. At what was to be his final meal the Buddha asked his blacksmith, Chanda, for food. Chanda placed the meat in Buddha's bowl and it was eaten. As mendicant monks, they ate anything they were given, including meat which was a major part of their diet.

The vegetarian diet is encouraged in Zen Buddhism to motivate compassion, but is not a requirement. In fact, vegetarianism emerged during the time of Pythagoras (570-495 BCE), a Greek philosopher and mathematician, and he is seen as the first and father of vegetarianism. There is some debate on whether Pythagoras ate fish (which is now classified as pescatarian) but he was the first who did not eat meat. Pythagoras taught his followers to avoid being cruel to all animals, but he also recognized the health benefits of a diet that is meat free. They were often persecuted for this thinking by the gladiators, so they kept silent. Vegetarians were called Pythagoreans until the late nineteenth century. Most Tibetan and

Japanese Buddhists eat some meat, and that includes His Holiness the Dalai Lama.

After the meal, the Buddha instructed his monks to bury the food and thanked Chanda. During his last Dharma class, Buddha told his sangha of his imminent parinirvana. After teaching the Dharma for decades, the Buddha's final words informed the sangha to experience rather rely on words of anyone, to be compassionate and to seek liberation from suffering. The Dharma taught by Buddha after his death was preserved by word of mouth because in 868 CE this was 600 years before the Gutenberg Bible was even produced.

As written by a Tibetan Geshe, Michael Roche
in his book *The Diamond Cutter*:

"In the beginning, it was passed down by word of mouth and then it (Buddha's words) was inscribed onto long palm leaves. These were durable fronds of palm on which the words of the book were first scratched, using a needle. Then charcoal dust was rubbed into the scratches left by the needle. The loose palm leaves would be kept together by a hole being bored with an awl through the middle of the stack of leaves and a string passes through the middle to keep the pages together. At first the Diamond Cutter was taught by Buddha in Sanskrit then later translated into Tibetan."

Bodhidharma
28th Patriarch & Father of Zen

The man from legendary Buddhist history and known as the Father of Zen is a monk known as Bodhidharma. There is little documentation, if any, on his life and deeds, but we learn his teachings from fables and philosophy as he carried them from his homeland, which was probably India to China and eventually Japan. During a Rohatsu Dharma class there could be a discussion of some of these legends. Bodhidharma is dated by modern scholars to the fifth century and credited as bringing Zen to China. As the 28th Patriarch of Buddhism, in a direct line to Gautama Buddha, he was ordained and a monk.

The first fascinating story is an exchange with Emperor Wu of Liang as he entered China:

Wu: *How much Karma merit have I earned for ordaining Buddhist monks, building monasteries, having sutras copied and commissioning Buddha images?*

Bodhidharma: *None. Good deeds done with worldly intent bring good karma, but no merit.*

31

That exchange was not well received, so the Indian or possibly Persian spiritual leader known as Bodhidharma traveled to a cave where he is said to have meditated for nine years while facing the wall. He did not speak to anyone, he simply meditated facing the wall which came to be known as wall gazing. There are many tales of Bodhidharma falling asleep and removing his own eyelids after seven years of meditation and then watching his eyelids fall and sprout tea he drank tea to stay awake.

The fables and tales increase interest in the legend, but it was his work at the Shaolin Temple that is taught multidisciplinary. The monks of the Shaolin Temple where Bodhidharma taught meditation were weak with atrophied legs and ill from disease. He got them up for exercise, resulting in the Kung Fu traditions of this group and their meditation teacher. Bodhidharma taught the monks of Shaolin Eighteen Arhat Hands — the forms included methods of elbow, palms, legs, and joint locking exercises. This was around 527 CE, he taught the Shaolin monks because they were terribly frail and falling asleep during meditation. The specific physical exercises combine energy and mindfulness and have emerged in modern day as Kung Fu. The word Lohan or Luohan is a Sanskrit word meaning Arhat. The top of the monk group 18 Arhats from Theravada were honored.

Bodhidharma's Zen practice focused on the Lankavatara Sutra, direct teachings from the Buddha involving everything from objects, names and forms, to manifestations of the mind. Bodhidharma was the 28th patriarch in a line from the Buddha.

Buddhism Divides
Theravada, Mahayana, Tibetan Book of the Dead

Zen emerged from Mahayana Buddhism, one of the major vehicles known as the *great vehicle*. There are many well-known schools, with Theravada and Mahayana being two of them, and various subsets under them or those that stand alone. Mahayana tradition has the written Pali canon in addition to scriptures and emphasizes bodhisattvas. Theravada teaches the concept of the Arhat with most emphasis on no Buddha nature in its teachings, but rather a goal of his personal enlightenment and end of his personal suffering. The Arhat is enlightened and has understood the Noble Path by eliminating desires and cravings as outlined. The Arhat also uses the Pali Canon and emphasizes rules and education. Mahayana, on the other hand, has its ideal as the Bodhisattva to help all sentient beings in a compassionate way, emphasizing intuition and practice. The Pali Canon is used in addition to scriptures.

All of the different vehicles of Buddhism came out of the councils that formed to discuss how to go forward after the death of the Buddha, since Buddhism has no central text as is common in other religions or philosophies. After the Buddha died and entered parinirvana, he was cremated and his ashes went to eight stupas, or burial monuments.

The Dharma, as he taught it for many years, should have left his monks well equipped to carry on his work. However, as in life, now there was a difference of opinion between the monks and heated discussions on changes or status quo, which resulted in a council meeting of all the monks. This first Council was called by Buddha's disciple Mahakessapa.

The First Council

Council I was held at Rajagriha, India and included 500 monks. Ananda, who had traveled with and spent most of his life with the Buddha and Opal, was designated the keeper of the rules. There was no written word at this point in history, so Ananda repeated Buddha's teachings again and again for all to memorize. This oral tradition of the Dharma was carried back to Sanghas by all of his monks. There is no written proof of this council.

The Second Council

Council II was held in Vasali. It was large, with 700 Arhats, and many disagreed about the precepts and need for more liberal or conservative interpretation. The end result was a split — a huge split that some call a session of the two large groups. So, 100 years after the death of the buddha, the Mahayana and Theravada split and Buddhism emerged. During the 2nd Council the Mahayana Zen accepted the concept of the Bodhisattvas that included Samantabhadra, Mizo, Manjushri and Avalokiteshvara.

Bodhisattva

A Bodhisattva finds joy in bodhicitta, the enlightened mind. Compassionate and empathic, they extend compassion to help all sentient beings. Bodhi means awakening and Citta in Sanskrit a conscious mind. Sanskrit is a classical language used in Buddhist texts. It dates back to 3300 BCE.

Manjushri is the Bodhisattva of transcendent wisdom, depicted usually as male with a flaming sword in his right hand cutting ignorance. He sits on a lion rather than fighting him. He is depicted with a sword that cuts down ignorance through ego and duality as a noble giant. As a genius himself, Manjushri helps with learning skills and memory. In his other hand he holds paramita, including the Diamond and Heart Sutras on a lotus stem, keeping the books of perfection and wisdom close to him.

Jizo is the guardian of children, women in childbirth and travel, offering a peaceful passage. Jizo Bosatsu guards children and travelers. The Jizo replicas are made out of stone for longevity and found on trails with more stones piled near them. Children who predecease their parents have difficulty crossing the afterlife rivers. Jizo statues are also used for childbirth and helping parents have good fertility. The Jizo replicas wear red hat and bibs because in Japan red protects against illness and fights evil. In *Super Mario Bros 3*, Mario and Luigi were able to turn to stone and become immortal statutes, which was inspired by the Jizo powers. The little Jizo stone statues are helped to do their work by people placing small stones and stonewalls near or above the statues.

Samantabhadra is the Bodhisattva or meditation and Buddhist practice. He is described in the Lotus Sutra. Together with Manjushri they are depicted as sitting to either side of the Buddha. There is a white elephant underneath, perhaps to honor Buddha's mothers dream of her conception. Three significant vows attributed to Samantabhadra include: (1) vowing to rejoice in other's merits, (2) to follow the teachings of Buddha at all times, and (3) to give generously.

Avalokitesvara in Sanskrit is the Mahayana Zen Buddhist bodhisattva of compassion. He is depicted as male with chest armor and sometimes facial hair. This bodhisattva is usually vegetarian due to his compassion. In China the name changes to Quan Yin and she is depicted as carrying pure water and willow branches dresses in beautiful white robes. The Jesuit missionaries nicknamed this saint the *mercy goddess*. The Lotus Sutra teaches us that chanting their name will free all from suffering. There are many names for the same bodhisattva and in Japan it is Kannon — the name of this revered compassionate changes from country to country but the respect remains constant.

The Third and Fourth Councils

Council III was in Pataliputra and called by King Ashoka 135 years after Council II. Council IV was in the first century, probably in Pakistan. There were 500 monks and also a second Council in Sri Lanka where the Theravada Buddhists wrote the Pali Canon in Pali (instead of Sanskrit) on palm leaves.

Tibetan Buddhism pre-dates the Dalai Lama, appearing as early as the seventh-ninth century under King Detsen. A woman named Yeshe Tsogyal in the king's court achieved enlightenment and taught the Dharma. It was long after Mahayana and Theravada Buddhism that Tibetan Buddhism ordained its first Dalai Lama Pema Dorje in 1405 CE. He was never aware of this title and it wasn't formally used for another hundred years. The 14th Dalai Lama Tenzin Gyats is the leader of Gelug known as yellow hats, in modern day Tibetan Buddhism.

All of the Dalai Lamas are thought to be reincarnations of Avalokitesvara the Bodhisattva of Compassion. There are many similarities and differences between the three major divisions of Buddhism, as there are with all philosophies and religions. In Tibetan Buddhism, which is more mystical, there are rituals that are meditative such as constructing mandalas, and the use of musical instruments during meditations, which departs from zazen for example. Tibetan practitioners repeat mantras such as *Om Mani Padme Hum*. The use of single point meditation is also used to provide structure to the meditation process focusing on a single object. This is called Samatha.

Tibetan Buddhism provides direction from the "*Bardo Thodol*" or the "*Tibetan Book of the Dead*," explaining the stages of death. The Tibetan book of the rituals teach that 49 days after a person dies is the first stage. This is not considered a time to cry, but rather it is believed loved ones should pray and talk to the deceased because recently dead have some level of consciousness in this realm and the dead are adjusting to their process and first stage. Prayers are heard and help the transition. At 49 days the loved ones cry and mourn their loss, then at 100 days there is a celebration of the person's life.

Ashoka
King of India & Buddhist Convert

The King of India named Ashoka was thought of as the man who spread the *Buddhist Path* from India to other countries surrounding this area.

H.G. Wells explains: *"Amidst the tens of thousands of names of monarchs that crowd the columns of history, their majesties and graciousnesses and serenities and royal highnesses and the like, the name of Ashoka shines, and shines, almost alone, a star. From the Volga to Japan his name is still honored. China, Tibet, and even India, though it has left his doctrine, preserve the tradition of his greatness."*

Ashoka (264 to 227 BCE), one of the great monarchs of history, whose dominions extended from Afghanistan to Madras, was the only military monarch on record in his day who abandoned warfare after victory. He had invaded Kalinga (255 BCE), a country along the East coast of Madras, perhaps with some intention of completing the conquest of the tip of the Indian peninsula. The expedition was successful, but he was disgusted by what be saw of the cruelties and horrors of war.

Ashoka declared, in certain inscriptions that still exist, that he would no longer seek conquest by war, but by religion, and the rest of his life was devoted to the spreading of Buddhism throughout the world.

"He seems to have ruled his vast empire in peace and with great ability. He was no mere religious fanatic. For eight and twenty years Ashoka worked sanely for the real needs of men. More living men cherish his memory today than have ever heard the names of Constantine or Charlemagne."
—H. G. Wells, in *The Outline of History (1920)*

Ashoka built 84,000 Stupas to hold the relics of Buddha. The Stupas were also places where people could meditate. The people of the entire Mauryan Empire were able to read his edicts carved in stone on fifty-foot pillars:

* Tolerance and understanding of all religions, as they are all pure of heart.

* Digging of wells for irrigation and trees planted for shade.

* More comfortable travel for both humans and animals.

* No human or animal sacrifices permitted.

* Building of hospitals and orphanages and medical care for all.

* Education of women.

* Kindness to prisoners including a three day wait of appeal by relatives on behalf of the convicted.

* Promoted vegetarianism.

* Directed the third Buddhist council.

* All subjects as equals to each other.

* Edicts of Ashoka a collection of 33 inscriptions on the pillars and cave walls so all could learn a better life under teachings and path of Buddhism.

The Ashoka pillar at Sarnath has four lions and has become the national emblem of India.

Ashoka died at age 72 and most of his ideas and edicts were reversed by the rulers who came after him, including the destruction of many cave edicts, pillars and stupas in war-torn modern-day countries.

His ability to spread the Dharma did not die with him, as evidenced by the practice of Buddhism in many of the countries where he sent Buddhist missionaries, especially after his son Mahindra translated Buddhist Canon to the native languages.

Zen Master Bankei
The Unborn Buddha Mind

Zen Master Bankei contributed more to Zen than any other seventeenth century teacher. Bankei Yotaku was born in 1622 and died in 1693, and worked toward enlightenment from a young age. Bankei's mother was seen in her day as a modern day mother of three potential Buddhas for the contributions her children made to Buddhism. After the death of his Samurai father, at a young age Bankei went to live with friends in a hut where he posted a sign: "Practice Hermitage."

Bankei studied Shin Buddhism, Sutras and Shingon since Buddhism itself had no holy book. At age 24 he was diagnosed with tuberculosis and prepared to enter parinirvana. However, as fate would have it he gained insight from his illness and began to meditate on his major idea of the "unborn." He spent a great deal of time in a Chinese temple but refused to chant in Chinese — instead requesting the chants to be in the language of the common people in the region.

Bankei's contribution was the concept of *The Unborn Mind,* which meant that we are all born in a state of

Buddhahood. However, our anxieties and projections take us out of the present and away from the unborn mind. Mindfulness is the key to staying present and avoiding the anxieties of wondering if we remembered to lock our front door while we are on the ski slopes, in a modern day analogy.

Bankei had the philosophy that the Precepts were made for monks who failed to follow the rules and therefore not needed for those following Buddhahood. He was progressive in his thinking and unorthodox. As Bankei explains in the *Unborn Mind,* we hear and see all things with an innate unborn mind without consciously trying to hear them. For example, we hear firetrucks or birds from the moment of our birth. Our perceptions begin to change as we grow into adults, creating a sense of anxiety around thoughts. People move toward exploring themselves in an effort to find home-base. This can create bad thoughts and habits and ultimately suffering.

The original face of the Unborn Buddha Mind is where we find the ability to exit our bad habits and thoughts by simply stepping back and observing them. Detaching from sad or happy and practicing equanimity moves this process toward Buddha Mind by not allowing it to slip away.

Bankei also took a radical approach toward respecting women's potential for Buddha Mind equal to men, which was not the common practice in the seventeenth century. Bankei wrote and taught in his Dharma class: *"You women, listen closely now. While in terms of physical form men and women are obviously different, in terms of Buddhamind there's no difference at all. Don't be misled by appearance! The Buddha Mind makes no distinction between men and women."*

Missionary Jesuits
Ignatius & Xavier Spreading Zen

Early in the sixteenth century, a Spanish priest named Saint Ignatius of Loyola created a spiritual system of exercises to enhance individual participation in establishing transformative spirituality. The meditations were suggested to be taught by a spiritual mentor or theologian over a period of several weeks in a retreat setting. All were invited to participate, including lay people. Saint Ignatius later became the founder of the Jesuits. Spiritual exercises required silence and solitude, but discernment is at the core of the exercises, the choice of ethical thought in making the correct choices between right and wrong.

While practicing the spiritual exercises in the retreat setting of solitude, Ignatius wrote that we should question in a classic contemplative way some questions which he calls *"application of the senses"* (Puhl, 121-126). Ignatius suggested we should: *"Ask yourself, 'What do I see? What do I hear? What do I feel, taste and smell?'"* (Martin, 2016). In the second exercise Loyola says: *"I will call to memory all the sins of my life, looking at them year by year or period by period. For these three things will be helpful: first, the locality of house where I lived; second, the associations which I had with others; third, the occupation I was pursuing. I will ponder looking at the foulness and evil if it were not forbidden."*

Spiritual exercises are a traditional and classic way to delve into a more spiritual life. They were from the year 1545. There are thousands of spiritual retreats run around the world asking many of the same questions as to how can I transform into a more spiritual life; in their case Saint Ignatius was both spiritual and religious. Loyola was the primary source for these ideas and the implementation of the program.

Loyola said, on the subject of eating: *"While one is eating one can use a different consideration, drawn from a life of some pious contemplation, or some spiritual project at hand. When the attention is thus directed to some good object, a person will be less concerned with the sensible pleasure from the bodily food. Above all, one should be on guard against being totally absorbed in what one is eating or letting oneself be completely dominated by the appetite. Rather, one should be master of oneself, both in the manner of eating and the amount one takes."* The most significant exercise is planning for the next day and meal: *"To rid oneself of disordered excess it is very profitable, after dinner or supper or at some other hour when the appetite to eat or drink in not strong, to settle with ones self how much food is to be taken at the next dinner or supper. Then, one should not exceed this amount either because of appetite and of temptation of disordered appetite."* With many diets today certainly lacking in mindfulness, Loyola nearly five-hundred years ago presented a very mindful approach.

Who was Ignatius? He was born in Spain and lost his mother shortly after birth, so he was raised by the help of his family. As a teen he joined the army in order to see the world and serve his country. During battle his legs were hit by a cannonball and he was returned to his father's home for treatment and recuperation. While receiving medical care, he began to read for the first time in his life and a spiritual conversion was in its early stages. Ignatius elected to study more of his religion and elected to read about meditations called *simple contemplations* that suggested visualization. Thus his transformation from vain glorious soldier to spiritual guide began. There are similarities to Ashoka's transformation to spirituality.

Ignatius Loyola learned the process of discernment and values of using the heart and mind to make better choices. Ignatius joined the Benedictine monastery of Santa Maria in Monserrat to examine his past transgressions and lifestyle. He was as a young man a ladies man and liked to party. This introspection led to what many before him have done as they become more self-actualized and spiritual.

Ignatius gave up his expensive clothes to the poor, and his accumulated wealth and dramatically placed his sword at the Virgin's altar. Ignatius went into a long period of solitude, praying in a cave in the grotto and practicing asceticism. He lived as a beggar, ate and drank sparingly and wore a sackcloth. Loyola's spiritual awakening was on the banks of the Cardoner River — the eyes of his understanding began to open and without seeing any vision, he understood and knew many things, as well spiritual things and things of faith (Olin, 30).

During this period of introspection, Ignatius decided to pursue an education; first elementary studies, then university and finally a master's degree from College of Sainte-Barbe, University of Paris at the age of 43. He was ordained a Catholic priest and lived his life teaching about the spiritual process. His spiritual quest for better understanding of making the correct choices in ethical versus moral decisions enhanced his life. This information is included on his history to again inform that the process of spirituality is transformative for the purpose of changing and becoming more human and working toward full potential. Ignatius founded the Jesuits.

Loyola's friend Francis Xavier was younger and offered to travel the world as a missionary for the Jesuits. He went to India where he was very well received. He taught spiritual concepts and interacted is a positive way with members of the Buddhist spiritual groups in the countries he visited including Japan, Cambodia, Maluku Islands, Vietnam, Thailand, Sri Lanka, and Myanmar. There is a preponderance of evidence to indicate that while in India, Xavier was credited for calling the Buddhist spiritual texts scripture.

Buddhism and the ideas now presented as Buddhist spirituality owe much to the Jesuits missionaries in general, up until 1550 when the Jesuits for the most part were responsible for teaching much of the Buddhist spiritual history in the various educational institutions. At the time of Loyola's death, the Jesuits had followers in Italy, Spain, Portugal, Japan, Germany, France, India, Congo and Ethiopia. Loyola wrote the structure and sent missionaries to many countries. The core of his program concluded that being highly educated all the way up to the university levels and graduate school can be an essential component on the journey to a greater spiritual understanding.

On scruples: *"A person who desires to make progress in the spiritual life ought always to proceed in a manner contrary to that of the enemy. In other words, if the enemy seeks to make a soul lax, it should try to make itself more sensitive. In the same way, if the enemy seeks to make a soul too sensitive, in order to entice it to an extreme, the soul should endeavor to establish itself staunchly in a correct mean and thus arrive at complete peace."*

This is the middle position to all aspects of life.

Zen Moves Toward Europe & America

There is documentation that Alexander the Great (334 BCE) had contact with the monks of Buddha Siddhartha Gautama around 380 BCE, but it was much later 1550-1950 that Europeans learned most of the Buddhist concepts, precepts and liturgy from the disciples of Ignatius Loyola. The missionaries of the Jesuits traveled into Japan and many countries such as Sri Lanka, Myanmar, Thailand and Tibet and then documented their respect for their spiritual friends, the Zen Buddhists. Nicolo Lanoill in 1588 and Francis Xavier in 1552 were amongst the most informative. Xavier wrote to Saint Ignatius Loyola in January of 1549 and June of 1552, that Buddhists had a hierarchy or leadership, they had orders of brothers, they gave sermons and most importantly they had a unique way to meditate. Many Jesuits became Zen meditators.

American intellectual elites in the 1820s Henry David Thoreau and Ralph Waldo Emerson were also learning of Zen Buddhism and enjoyed meditation. In 1850, California experienced a gold rush, attracting prospectors to the Western Coast of the United States. It also attracted immigration from China to work for the prospectors and Chinese Zen monks to attend to the spiritual needs of these immigrants. It is interesting to note the word Buddhism did not even appear in English language dictionaries until 1812. By 1853, California saw the first Zen Buddhist Temple. Hawaii also received many Zen Buddhists by 1868 from Japan.

Unfortunately, laws were passed first in 1882 limiting immigration to qualified Chinese and in 1906 separate but equal schools for Asian Immigrants and Asian Americans by the California Board of Education. These practices were noticed by Soyen Shaku when he came to America for the World Parliament of Religions in 1893. The Parliament of World Religions was attended by Soyen Shaku representing Zen and Anagarika Dharmapala representing Theravada. It was mostly attended by Unitarian and Protestant denominations, as well as Buddhists from the East.

Today there are over 1,000 Buddhist Temples with 350 being Theravada. That includes Tassajara Zen Mountain Center, which was the first Zen monastery in the USA in 1966 and is in California. It was founded by Suzuki Roshi. The largest Buddhist Temple, called

Hsi Temple, was built in Hacienda Heights, California in 1991 and was founded by monks from Taiwan.

A Bowl of Tea
Respect, Purity, Tranquility, Harmony

The Japanese Tea Ceremony is called Chado and means the *Way of Tea*. It is the ceremonial preparation and serenity of the traditions that inform us Chado is the ceremonial quintessential spiritual experience to be repeated exactly in form and as frequently as possible to ensure it takes its place as a portal to our spiritual existence.

The tea ceremony expresses the simplicity of Zen and was initiated by Sen no Rikyu in the early 1500s. He brought a simple, totally austere method of spiritual mindfulness to the sharing of a cup of tea. Chado is frequently used during a Rohatsu sesshin. The ceremony is held in a tearoom, usually in the center of a fragrant and beautiful natural garden. The entrance to the tea room includes the Shinto practice of washing hands and mouth to purify before entering. After walking into the tearoom through the shoji sliding doors, one is greeted by the scent of freshly picked flowers and the beauty of their presence. The entrance itself is low level, so guests must bend which is a symbol of humility and everyone being equal in the way of tea, as in life. The floor is constructed of tatami mats made from woven straw of about two meters. The tables are low and the guests sit on a zabuton.

The Tea Master carries the tea bowl and whisk, scoop, napkin and tea. Tea Master has also placed the fresh water on the fire to boil in advance of the ceremony. The waste water has a container which holds the ladle and is placed in position. Each step is done according to a rigidly traditional format for the expressed purpose of a ceremonial meditation that includes respect, purity, tranquility, and harmony.

Step one: Tea Master uses a cloth and wipes the tea scoop and container, indicating to all present that cleanliness exemplifies purity.

Step two: Using the ladle, the tea master scoops hot water from the kettle and places it in the tea bowl with the whisk for cleaning, then pours it into the waste container and wipes clean and dries everything.

Step three: The powdered tea called matcha is whipped. Tea Master ceremoniously picks up the tea in the left hand and the scoop is picked up in the right hand and three scoops of matcha is placed in the tea bowl.

Step four: The hot water is poured on the matcha and whisked and then placed in the tea masters left palm. The Tea Master, then holding the tea bowl with the right hand, turns it two full turns until the front of the bowl is now facing guests. The first guest picks up the bowl and holds it as the tea master did.

Step five: The guest holding the tea bowl cup turns toward the second guest and they gassho back and forth. This is a "here you first... no you go first" politeness and the second guest declines. Raising the bowl in a bow to the tea master, the first guest then sips tea. After savoring the tea with use of all a sentient being can use, the guest respectfully concludes by cleaning the bowl with thumb and finger or a cloth if it is available.

Step six: The tea bowl can be repeated down the line or handed back to the tea master for the process to be repeated after cleaning, or handed down the line until the last guest or member of the sangha has had tea.

Step seven: Reverse the process and clean all instruments and bowls and place them in their appropriate place. This process is repetitive and meditative.

Drinking tea is healthy due to polyphenols, which are antioxidants that neutralize free radical damage from the sun, pollution and bad diet. The most important polyphenols are catechins. The other component of tea that is most helpful is L-theanine — an amino acid which produces a gradual exposure to caffeine in tea creating a more gently serene experience rather than the more immediate impact of other caffeinated beverages.

Urasenke Grand Master XV offered this message on the Chado: *"Served with a respectful heart and received with gratitude, a bowl of tea satisfies both physical and spiritual thirst."*

Zen Poetry: Haiku
Ichi-go Iche-e

Ichi-go iche-e... One time, one meeting, the unrepeatable nature in the moment. The view is irreplicable, once in a lifetime, so give it undivided attention before writing the haiku. Life, by its very nature, is impermanent. It is that impermanence that makes us rejoice at the sight of beauty in natural settings. The philosophy of Japanese Zen is consistent with haiku enthusiasts, making them a perfect match with this form of poetry. The elder haiku writers appreciated the impermanence of the scenes in nature and felt that moment would be gone in an instant, making it even more beautiful. Many early haiku poets were Buddhists in the Zen tradition, where haiku was an expressive art. Zen emphasizes staying in the present. The form of three lines of five, seven and five syllables make haiku poetry the short expression of nature and seasonal change. It permits the person reading to interpret the meaning.

Haiku does not require any special technique or equipment, as with most art. The simple tools of pen and paper enable anyone, anywhere to be a poet. Haiku is three short little lines in a small poem that speaks volumes about how we think while viewing nature. We connect our true feelings of things in nature with a hint of the season and how we perceive it. Once touched by the words in the haiku poem, our feelings flow in free association. Haiku is seeing beauty in nature and then expressing it in the written word describing how we feel about it. Haiku takes place in the present, a moment in time.

A Historical Perspective of Haiku Poetry

Matsuo Basho was born Matsuo Chuemon Munefusa in 1644 in Edo or modern Tokyo. Basho was the world's greatest haiku writer. He was born into a Samurai family but elected to become a teacher in Edo and joined the intellectual world rather than the military. He wrote what was then called *Hokku*. He took the pen name of Sobo, which is a Sino-Japanese nickname for Munefusa, and was first published at age 20. Basho left teaching and started a journey into the wilderness on what was called *Edo Five Routes* or 5 highways between Tokyo and Kyoto, which at the time was very dangerous. It was as if after facing his fears on these dangerous paths that he was finally happy. He practiced Zen meditation. His trips took him to Kyoto and Mt. Fuji and he was able to observe the seasons, so his writing became less introspective and more about nature. Basho eventually returned back to his home area to teach but continued writing haiku. Basho occasionally entertained muses, but seemed to grow reclusive and preferred his huts alone. Finally in 1694 he became sick with a stomach issue, which was his fatal illness. The similarities to Siddhartha or the historical Buddha are fascinating and of course Zen was a part of Basho's life so he did study the Buddhist teachings.

Basho's last poem:
Falling sick on a journey
my dream goes
wandering
over a field of dried grass

By the 1800s the Shinto culture of Japan had deified Basho, so everyone had to love him, but most would have anyway. The one exception to come along was Masaoka Tsunenori, or his pen name, Shiki.

Shiki was born September 17, 1867, and was writing poetry by age 15. He was expelled from middle school due to his radical ideology and quit college. He was with the Japanese army as a correspondent during the Sino-Japanese War and returned home to write poetry after serving in the military. Shiki was very influenced by the Western style of poetry writing. He felt poetry should be about things as they are in reality. He wrote in contemporary speech and placed haiku in the category of literature. The word *HAIKU* was first introduced to us by Shiki. He felt hokku should be used as the indication of the opening verse of renku. He was a prolific writer of haiku but unfortunately his case of tuberculosis worsened and he died young at age 34. Shiki had two students, Kyoshi, who felt haiku should contain poetry about nature and Hekigodo, the other student who felt it could be about any subject.

Taniguchi Yosa Buson (1716-1784). Buson was a leading painter and haiku writer from Edo and Kyoto. His haiku was impressionistic but maintained haiku rules. Tan Taigi and Kuroy Ngi Shoha helped Buson develop spontaneous style even though their styles were very different. He became the central figure of a haiku revival known as the return to Basho movement. Buson's group built a Basho Hut for haiku and linked verse gatherings. Buson created many illustrated scrolls and screens including text of *Oku,* which helped canonize Basho as a grand saint of poetry. Yosa married, had a child, and lived to 68.

Kobayashi Issa (1762-1826). Issa was a sensitive man and ordained as a Buddhist priest of the Pure Land tradition. Issa means "cup of tea." He wrote of nature's imperfections in his haiku. Issa faced many tragedies including the death of his mother at three and then the death of his wife and children. He was a prolific artist as well as a poet.

"The Buddhism of the haiku contrasts with the Zen of the sketch"
-Issa, from *A History of Haiku, Volume One*

Issa is quoted in JD Salinger's 1961 novel *Franny and Zooey*:

O snail
Climb Mount Fuji
But slowly, slowly!

These poetic giants were opening the gates of possibilities in both Japan and America.

Haiku Style

Traditional haiku has some key elements: Kigo, Kireji, Saijiki and Kiru.

Kigo is the traditional haiku reference to the season. The kigo alludes to the season. For example spring might be young grass, cherry blossoms, or frog peepers. Kigo are frequently in the metonyms or figures of speech that we use in place of the actual wording. It is the name of an association rather than its real name. An example would be Wall Street for financial services, Hollywood for the motion picture industry, the track for horse racing and a crown for the royal family.

Kiru is a cutting in the poem and the most important part of haiku. It separates the juxtaposition in the haiku.

Kireji in traditional haiku always has a cutting word that divides the poem into sections with the purpose of each section helping to accent the understanding. Many American haiku writers use a dash or ellipsis to substitute for kireji.

Saijiki is a reference pool from brainstorming a sort of dictionary for Kigo. It includes many trigger words from the seasons for use in the haiku. The seasonal haikus contain numerous references. In Japan they are divided according to the dates each season begins and ends.

Saijiki examples: SPRING — young love, pure, ethical, marriage, tranquil, serene, plow, herbs, silkworms, blossoms, azalea, buds, sprouts, nori, frogs. SUMMER — beach, sea, excess heat, sky blue, hot, south wind, fragrant breeze, evening downpour, thunder, drought, dripping waterfall, straw mats, rice planting, swimming, cutting grass, fireworks, airing, smog, cicada. FALL — loss, end of relationships, leaves changing, mysterious, autumn air, night chill, harvest moon, dew frost, mackerel clouds. WINTER — snow, ice, no leaves, loss, NYE, short day, no leaves, fireplace, bonfire, hawk, wood burning stove, porridge, seven herbs, cold, freezing, windy.

"Learn The Rules & Then Forget Them"
Haiku from Zen Japan to America...

In 1913 Ezra Pound published the first haiku written in English. It came from an experience he had in a Paris subway. The entire haiku was only 14 words — that in my opinion exemplifies the existential notion that life is of the nature of impermanence. The poem is called "In a Station of the Metro." Check it out and keep in mind that American haiku started with him. It is also interesting to make note of why some of Basho's poems quoted in this book do not appear to conform to the 5-7-5 suggested format.

Japanese haiku counts sounds, not syllables. The work haiku has two syllables in English but in Japanese it has three sounds. The word Tokyo has three syllables toe-key-oh in English but in Japanese toe-oh-kyo-oh has four sounds and basically four syllables. In "The Poetics of Japanese Verse," by Koji Sakamoto it is taught the word sign has one syllable but in Japanese three sounds sig-ya-n. In both Japanese and English we all agree that the word sushi has two sounds and two syllables, which makes me very happy because it is my favorite food and I enjoy including the word sushi in my poetry. The point of haiku is to convey feelings.

Basho said, "Learn the rules and then forget them." Sage advice.

Mindfulness & Spirituality

"Mindfulness is the substance of a Buddha. When you enter deeply into the present moment you too become a living Buddha. You see the nature of reality and this insight liberates you from suffering and confusion."
-Thich Nhat Hanh

Mindfulness is synergistic with Buddhist philosophy and is a non judgmental acceptance of the feelings that emerge in our thoughts and emotions, in the present. Mindfulness can manifest into a lifelong spiritual practice. It is cultivated from an intention to view things as they manifest in the moment to moment, not in the past or future. It is the interoceptive awareness that acts as the catalyst to dig deep inside our body to allow this transformation.

Mindfulness is also a state of conscious awareness of surroundings, unencumbered by judgmental attitudes and thoughts which tend to restrict the ability to place into context the attitudes and feelings in relation to the world as we find it, rather than the world we imagine we are in.

Spirituality is a uniquely individual experience resulting from an introspective assessment of the moral, ethical and compassionate components of our lives. It includes the non-materialistic aspects of life. Exploring one's spirituality is a transformative process of the core need for solitude and includes ethical and moral choices. A human's true self experiences personal growth during the contemplative process usually resulting in a more compassionate existence for themselves and others who they interact with during their lifetime.

Currently one-third of Americans define themselves as spiritual, not religious. Spiritual but not religious (SBNR) is an acronym used to describe this thirty percent. There are two perspectives defining spirituality: traditional and new age. In the fifteenth century the traditional concept of spirituality taught that religion was the path to personal growth by working toward becoming closer to the image of God.

Kabbalah as a school of thought of Judaism is a profoundly spiritual quest toward answering many of the ontological questions that exist. The study of being or ontology is explored by Islamic Sufism as a mystical spirituality. According to Sufi teacher Ahmad

Ibn Ajiba in his book *The Principles of Sufism,* "A *science through which one can know how to travel into the presence of the Divine, purify one's inner self and beautify it with a variety of praise worthy traits.*"

In early Christianity, spirituality was considered as a process to reform in the image of God and living out of a personal act of faith in the study of the Holy Spirit. After World War II in America, theistic and spiritual disconnected. It became a unique experience rather than in the past, everyone approached a more spiritual path by means of doctrines from organized religions.

The spiritual component to our daily lives is always a transformative path intended to create change as a result of spiritual practice.

Meditation Suggestions

Find a quiet place.

Eliminate distractions such as cell phones, television, and computers.

Choose a comfortable position, preferably one of the following:

- Upright on a chair
- On a cushion
- Cross-legged
- Lotus or Half-Lotus posture
- Burmese seated position
- Kneeling, supported by a cushion, or a seiza bench

Keep a straight back. Sit upright.

Breathing in through the nose, allowing the mouth to gently close, placing the tongue behind the front teeth and lowering the eyes. If needed, counting the breath can be helpful — counting one as inhale and exhale. Bowing hands together and bowing from the hip. The Anjali mudra with a slight bow and hands pressed together. Many Zens bow three times: showing devotion to the Buddha's mindfulness, then the Dharmas, and finally the Sangha itself.

Mala beads are used to assist in mantra meditation. They normally have 108 beads with one special one being called the guru bead. The mala beads are used in conjunction with the breath and mantra alternating to help maintain equanimity during the meditation. The use of the mala beads includes an understanding that the index finger is never used nor does it even touch the beads. This is a reminder that the index finger represents the ego and Buddhism is egoless.

The use of the mala beads follows a specific, essentially standard practice. Holding the mala in your right hand between the thumb and all of the fingers except the index finger — that finger simply points out. Once secure and in position, start with the guru bead and draw the beads toward you. Pull each bead toward you and on pulling the thumb forward inhale pull back then exhale. When you reach the guru bead, again, never cross over it — instead gently twist your right wrist toward your body extending your thumb under the guru bead so it slips the middle fingers under the beads. You are now moving in the opposite direction but did not pass over the guru bead.

Focus your attention on breathing or a mantra. A mantra can be a poem, prayer, phrase, chant or word such as *OM*.

Center breathing on the Hara line which is the line that runs vertically up the center of the body. If the mind wanders, bring it back to your breath or mantra.

Focus on positive thoughts and/or visualize a tranquil setting.

It may be helpful to set a timer if so desired for when it is time for you to re-enter full consciousness. Last, but not least, many of the world's ancient religions and spiritual practices involve voluntary acts of asceticism which is the avoidance of all forms of indulgence. They do this to reach spiritual goals for themselves and to have a positive effect on their communities.

My Personal Journey

While in college, I made a choice to study and learn how to meditate. It was during my days in academia, both college and graduate school, that I was first exposed to Zen meditation, which soon became my personal choice for a variety of reasons. The most important reason being chats with my mother's cousin who married, then lived in Japan. He spoke of most people being born Shinto and many spending their lives as Zen Buddhists in Japan due to the spirituality of zazen. Zen in the Mahayana tradition has been my choice over the years.

During my marriage to a Californian we flew out to visit his family frequently, until finally moving there while he pursued a fellowship at a medical school in Los Angeles. This afforded me wonderful opportunities to sit zazen in an area of the country that had multiple Zen monasteries and organizations. I enjoyed visiting *San Francisco Zen Center*.

Upon returning to the East Coast, I also found many Zen organizations and enjoyed participating in a few for Rohatsu sesshin. Of special interest were *Zen Mountain Monastery* and John Daido Loori's *Eight*

Gates in upstate New York. One extraordinary highlight while attending a seminar on meditation in New Jersey — Michael Carroll, who wrote *Awake at Work: 35 Practical Buddhist Principles for Discovering Clarity and Balance in the Midst of Work's Chaos*, sat near me. I did what Americans do, I asked for his autograph! As he started to write a note on some paper I presented a copy of his book from my purse complete with yellow highlighting. This amazing man, who is in the lineage of Tibetan meditation Master Chogyam Trungpa, invited me to his meditation seminar and to his table for lunch on that wonderful day of learning. Living in Pennsylvania, I also traveled with friends to enjoy the teachings of the His Holiness The Dalai Lama on several occasions when he presented seminars in Philadelphia.

For the past several decades I have enjoyed sitting zazen and Rohatsu with others like me; men and women who seek a more spiritual life. We are from all walks of life and many from faith based religions. We meet in various homes, or these days video-chat and sometimes attend one of the many authentic monasteries. We all purchased *Sangha in a Box* years ago from the Plum Village Thich Nat Hahn organization and follow the suggestions including listening to the Dharma classes. We just sit. We sit zazen. We sit together.

If you are reading this book with a plan to study Zen, I would like to suggest an excellent place to find ethical and ordained with transmission certified Zen centers as listed in this Zen association:

zenteachers.org

May I become at all times, both now and forever,

A protector for those without protection,

A guide for those who have lost their way,

A ship for those with oceans to cross,

A bridge for those with rivers to cross,

A sanctuary for those in danger,

A lamp for those without light,

A place of refuge for those who lack shelter,

And a servant to all in need.

by Shantideva, an eighth century Indian Buddhist monk

Resources

Bankei & Waddell, Norman (translator). *The Unborn: The Life and Teachings of Zen Master Bankei.* North Point Press, 2002.

Blyth, R.H. *A History of Haiku Volume One: From the Beginnings up to Issa.* Hokuseido Press, 1984.

Carroll, Michael. *Awake At Work: 35 Practical Buddhist Principles for Discovering Clarity and Balance in the Midst of Work's Chaos.* Shambhala, 2006.

Chodron, Pema. *When Things Fall Apart.* Shambhala, 1997.

Collcutt, Martin. *Five Mountains: The Rinzai Zen Monastic Institution in Medieval Japan.* Harvard University Asia Center, 1996.

D'Ecclesis, Nora. *Spiritual Portals: A Historical Perspective.* Blackstone Publishing, 2019. Audiobook.

Harvey, Peter. *An Introduction to Buddhism.* Cambridge University Press, 1990.

Kakuzo, Okakura. *The Book of Tea.* Running Press, 2002.

Loori, John Daido. *The Eight Gates of Zen.* Dharma Communications, 1992.

Martin, Fr. James. An Introduction to Ignatian contemplation. *American Magazine.* 21 September, 2016.

Nanamoli, Bhikkhu and Bodhi, Bhikkhu (translators). *The Middle Length Discourses of the Buddha.* Wisdom Publications, 1995.

Narada. *A Manual of Buddhism.* Buddhist Missionary Society, 1971.

Olin, John C. (Editor). *The Autobiography of Saint Ignatius Loyola.* Fordham University Press, 1993.

Puhl, Louis J. (translator). *The Spiritual Exercises of Saint Ignatius.* Loyola Press. 7 MARCH. 2017, pp. 121-126.

Roach, Geshe Michael. *The Diamond Cutter: The Buddha on Managing your Business and Your Life.* Doubleday, 2000.

Schumann, H.W. *The Historical Buddha: The Times, Life, and Teachings of the Founder of Buddhism.* Motilal Banarsidass, 2016.

Thich Nat Hanh. *Living Buddha, Living Christ.* Riverhead Books, 1995.

Thurman, A.F. Robert (translator). *The Tibetan Book of the Dead.* Bantam Books, 1994.

Watts, Alan. *The Way of Zen.* Vintage, 1999.

Acknowledgements

Deep Bows and acknowledgements to the meditation group.

We are a sangha with leadership provided by...
Dr. George Bonner, Dharma Teacher
Maria
Margaret Elaine
Janice
Richard S.

We sit together in community:
Chris, Greg, Cheryl, Michelle W., Barbara S., Karen I., Joan, Gwen, Rosalie, Terri, Sheri, Donna E., Diana, Theresa, Luke, Janis Cathleen, Cristin, Faye, Erica, Mark, Lauri, Rich H., Bonnie, Debra T., Ivanna, Michelle W., Monica, Colin B., Samantha, Ruth, Ronya, Donna L., Stacy Z., Robert, Michelle R., Tim, Colleen, Alanna, Angie, Karime, Tracy, Morgan, Wally, Susan, John Patrick, Amanda, Carrie, Stacy S., Michael, Janel, Cashee, and Marlene.

About The Author

Nora D'Ecclesis is an American bestselling and award winning non-fiction author. Her #1 Amazon Bestselling Audiobook *Spiritual Portals: A Historical Perspective,* published by Blackstone Audio Publishing is also available in ebook and paperback. *Multicultural Mindfulness: Nourishing the Soul* was a first place gold winner in the spring, 2022 *The BookFest* Award.

Nora's published non-fiction include bestseller *Haiku: Natures Meditation* and paperbacks/ebooks on topics such as time management, tick borne illness, a personal cyber security password log, guided visualizations, gratitude/equanimity journaling and zen meditation. Nora was the solo medalist in spirituality from the *New Apple Literary Award*. She added novelist to her list with the publication of *Twin Flames* written with her co-author, William Forstchen who is a NYT #1 bestselling novelist.

Nora is a graduate of Kean University. She has a long history of presenting events, retreats and seminars focused on wellness and stress reduction techniques. She enjoys kayaking and hiking. Nora lives with her family and wonderful dogs in a suburb of Philadelphia, Pennsylvania.

Made in the USA
Las Vegas, NV
05 September 2022

54724270R10059